THE MYSTERIOUS
Universe

Writer: Robin Kerrod
Designer: Tri-Art
Illustrators: Max Ansell, Gordon Davies, Philip Ems,
John Harwood, Len Huxter, Lee Noel, John Marshall
Cover Illustrator: John Marshall
Series Editor: Christopher Tunney
Art Director: Keith Groom

LIBRARY OF CONGRESS CATALOGING IN PUBLICATION DATA

Kerrod, Robin.
The mysterious universe.

(The Question and answer books)
Includes index.
SUMMARY: Presents questions and answers about the
universe, including the sun, moon, earth and other planets,
stars, and galaxies.

1. Astronomy—Juvenile literature. [1. Astronomy. 2. Questions
and answers] I. Title.

QB46.K42   1980   520   79-2345
ISBN 0-8225-1181-9   lib. bdg.

This revised edition © 1980 by Lerner Publications Company.
Published simultaneously in Canada by J. M. Dent & Sons (Canada) Ltd.,
Don Mills, Ontario.

First edition copyright © 1978 by Sackett Publicare Ltd.

International Standard Book Number: 0-8225-1181-9
Library of Congress Catalog Card Number: 79-2345

Manufactured in the United States of America.

1 2 3 4 5 6 7 8 9 10 85 84 83 82 81 80

The Question and Answer Books

THE MYSTERIOUS Universe

THE MYSTERIOUS

 Lerner Publications Company ▪ Minneapolis

THE NIGHT SKY The night sky has a beauty we can all enjoy. The stars sparkle like jewels on a velvet background. The Moon, always changing its shape, pours its silvery light into the darkness. At first sight, the night sky appears to be filled haphazardly with stars. But, after a while, we find that we can recognize patterns of stars and thus find our way through the heavens. By studying the heavens, we become astronomers. Astronomy is perhaps the oldest science of all. The Chaldeans and the Babylonians were skilled observers of the heavens over 5,000 years ago.

What are the constellations?

Constellations are the patterns the bright stars make in the sky. Ancient astronomers imagined they could see the shapes of animals, people, and other things in the pattern of the stars, and named the constellations accordingly. In astronomy the constellations are known by their Latin names, such as *Leo* (the Lion).

Pisces, the Fishes

Leo, the Lion

Scorpio, the Scorpion

Ursa Major, the Great Bear

Orion, the Hunter

Why do they move?

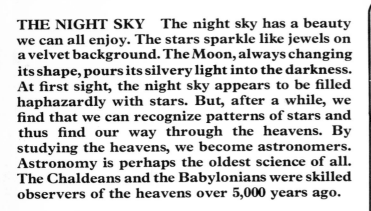

If you remain stargazing for long enough, you notice that the constellations move through the heavens hour by hour. In 24 hours they are more or less back where they started. This happens because the Earth is spinning in space, once every 24 hours. Ancient astronomers thought that the stars were fixed on the inside of a great celestial sphere that circled around the Earth.

Can we ever see all the constellations?

Which constellations you can see depends on where you are on Earth. The best place to be is near the Equator. There you can, over the year, see almost all the constellations. If you live elsewhere, there are some constellations you will never see.

Constellations of the Southern Hemisphere

Constellations of the Northern Hemisphere

The Zodiac

Throughout the year, the Sun, the Moon, and the planets appear to travel through a narrow band of the heavens. It is called the *zodiac*. There are 12 constellations along this band, called the *signs of the zodiac*. The positions of the heavenly bodies in the zodiac are thought by some people to influence our lives and future actions. This belief is the basis of astrology. Astrologers were very important people in ancient times.

What is the pole star?

The pole star is a star almost directly above the Earth's North Pole. This means that as the Earth spins, the pole star appears to stay in the same place. When you take a long-exposure photograph of the northern sky, the pole star appears as a dot. The other stars show up as arcs.

How big is the Moon?

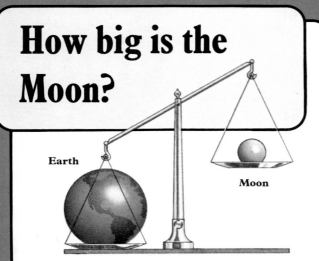

Earth

Moon

The Moon is very much smaller than the Earth. Its diameter is only about a quarter that of the Earth. If the Earth were hollow, you could fit nearly 50 Moons into it. Because it is small, the Moon has a small gravity. If you went to the Moon, you could jump six times higher than you can on Earth.

THE SILVER MOON The Earth and the Moon travel through space together. The Moon is the Earth's satellite. It circles around the Earth about once a month. Our word "month" comes from "moon." We know more about the Moon than about any other body in outer space. This is because men from Earth have actually landed on the Moon and explored its surface. They have brought back lunar soil and rocks. ("Lunar" means "of the Moon.") The Moon is by far the Earth's nearest neighbor in space. It lies only about 240,000 miles (385,000 km) away. This is just a stone's throw in space. The other heavenly bodies lie many millions of miles away.

What is the Moon's surface like?

The Moon is so close that we can see many details of its surface from Earth. The bright regions are rugged highlands covered with holes, or *craters*. The dark regions are flat, and are called *maria* (seas).

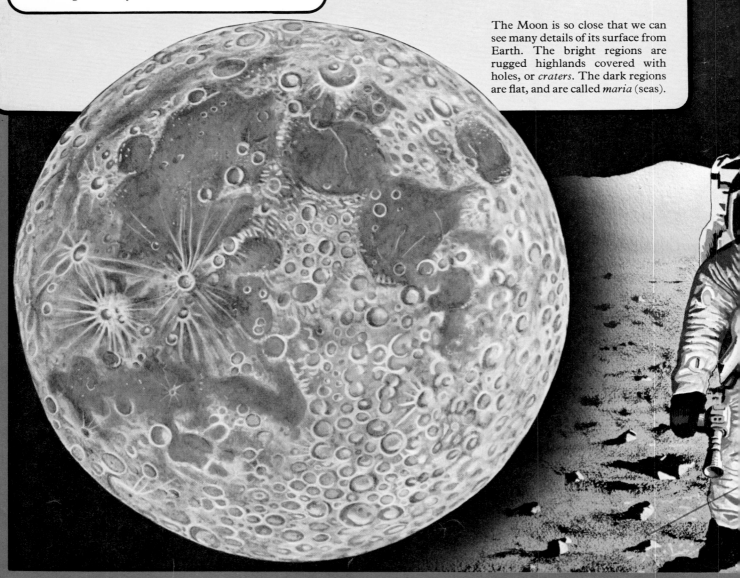

Why can we see only one side?

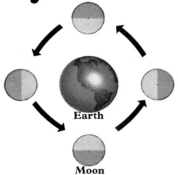

If you study the Moon from month to month, you notice that it keeps the same face toward us all the time. The reason is that the Moon spins on its own axis while it is traveling around the Earth. Every time it circles the Earth once, it spins once on its axis.

Why does the Moon change shape?

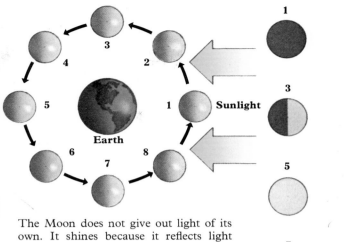

Moon's phases

The Moon does not give out light of its own. It shines because it reflects light from the Sun. As the Moon circles the Earth, the Sun lights up different parts of it. From Earth it looks as if the Moon is changing shape. We call these changing shapes the Moon's *phases*.

What is it like on the Moon?

The Apollo astronauts who visited the Moon found that it is a lifeless, barren wasteland. There is no air on the Moon, nor any water. It is scorching hot by day, and very cold at night. The surface is covered with dust, and there are rocks strewn around everywhere between the many craters.

7

THE SOLAR SYSTEM The Earth and the Moon belong to a family of bodies that travels through space with the Sun. We call this family the solar system. The most important members of the family are the nine bodies we call the planets. The Earth is a planet. In order of increasing distance from the Sun the other planets are: Mercury, Venus, (Earth), Mars, Jupiter, Saturn, Uranus, Neptune, and Pluto.

Who thought of a solar system?

In the third century, BC, a Greek astronomer called Aristarchus first suggested that the Earth revolved around the Sun, and not the other way around. But no one else believed this until a Polish priest, Nicolaus Copernicus (above), introduced the idea again in 1543.

How do the planets move?

The planets move in two different ways in space. One, they spin on their axes like tops. Two, they travel around the Sun in great oval paths, or *orbits*. Viewed from the north, they move counterclockwise.

How big are they?

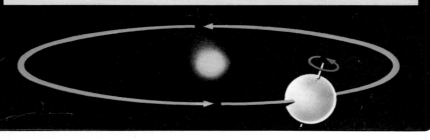

Mercury   Venus   Earth   Mars

Jupiter

The biggest planets by far are Jupiter and Saturn, which have diameters of 88,600 and 74,700 miles respectively (142,600 and 120,200 km). If Jupiter were hollow, it could swallow over 1,300 Earths; Saturn could swallow over 750. Uranus and Neptune are near twins, with diameters of about 31,000 miles (50,000 km). Next in size, but very much smaller, comes the Earth, followed by its neighbors Venus and Mars. The smallest of the planets is believed to be the one closest to the Sun—Mercury, with a diameter of only 3,015 miles (4,850 km). The outermost planet, Pluto, is also small, and may in fact be smaller than Mercury.

How far from Earth are the other planets?

None of the planets comes very near the Earth. Even the nearest, Venus, never gets closer than about 26 million miles (42 million km). This is over 100 times farther away than the Moon. The farthest planet, Pluto, never comes much closer than about 3,000 million miles (5,000 million km).

Pluto

Neptune

Uranus

Saturn

What else circles the Sun?

Many other bodies circle the Sun besides the planets. They include the *satellites*, or moons, which circle around the planets. There are also the shapeless lumps of rock that we call the *asteroids* or minor planets. There are even smaller bodies still, which we see in the night sky as *comets* and *meteors*.

Asteroid

THE LIFE-GIVING SUN (1) The Sun is our star. It is very much like millions of other stars in the sky. It appears bigger and brighter only because it is so very much closer to us. It lies 93 million miles (150 million km) away. It has a diameter of 865,000 miles (1,400,000 km)— about 115 times that of the Earth.

What is the Sun made of?

Like all ordinary stars, the Sun is a massive ball of white-hot gas. Most of it is hydrogen gas. If you could cut into the Sun, you would find that it would get hotter and hotter the deeper you went. The outer surface has a temperature of about 10,000°F (6,000°C). But in the center, the temperature is as high as 27,000,000°F. (15,000,000°C). We call the visible surface of the Sun the *photosphere* ("light-sphere").

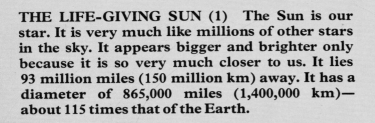

How does the Sun affect us?

The Sun affects everything on Earth in one way or another. It gives the Earth heat, light, and life. Plants need the energy in sunlight to make food, and we all rely on plant life to live. Fuels exist thanks to the Sun, since they are plant remains. The Sun causes our weather, because it heats the air, the land, and the oceans.

Why does the Sun turn red at sunset?

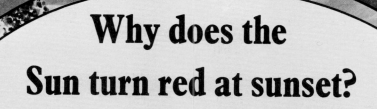

When the Sun is low in the evening sky, it often appears blood-red. This happens because of dust in the atmosphere. The dusty atmosphere acts as a kind of filter, which lets through mainly red light. A red night often means that the following day will be clear.

The Sun is all-important to life on Earth, and practically all ancient peoples worshipped it as a god. The ancient Egyptians named their Sun-god *Ra*. The Greeks and Romans named him *Apollo*. The Aztecs of Mexico, the Incas of Peru, and the Mayas of Central America were also Sun worshippers.

Why does the Sun shine?

The Sun is like a huge atomic furnace. It "burns" atoms of hydrogen in its very hot center. The atoms fuse, or combine, to form atoms of helium. When this happens, great amounts of energy are given out as light and heat. Humans have imitated this process in the terrifying hydrogen bomb.

Will the Sun always shine?

The Sun will continue to shine as it does now for another 5,000 million years. Then it will swell into a red giant star so large that it will extend beyond the Earth's orbit. It will then shrink into a white dwarf star little bigger than the Earth.

What is the Sun's surface like?

The surface is a sea of white-hot gas. Here and there, tongues of flaming gas, or *flares*, shoot upward. Sometimes, great fountains of gas erupt and are hundreds of thousands of miles high. We call them *prominences*. On some parts of the surface, there are dark regions that we call *sunspots*. They are cooler than the rest of the surface.

What is an eclipse?

An eclipse is what happens when one heavenly body moves into the shadow cast in space by another. An eclipse of the Sun occurs when the Moon moves in between the Sun and the Earth. It casts a tiny shadow on the Earth.

An eclipse of the Moon occurs when the Moon moves into the shadow cast in space by the Earth. Because the Earth is quite large compared with the Moon, it casts a big shadow. The Moon can spend up to $2\frac{1}{2}$ hours in this shadow.

What is a total eclipse?

A total eclipse occurs when the Moon's disk exactly covers the disk of the Sun. At the beginning of an eclipse, the Moon starts to cover the bright Sun. Daylight fades into twilight. At the moment of total eclipse, day suddenly turns into night for up to 7 minutes. Then the sky brightens as the Sun reappears.

Ancient peoples used to fear eclipses. The Chinese thought a huge dragon was trying to swallow the Sun. They made a great noise to frighten it away. It always worked!

How did the Sun form?

The Sun was born from a great cloud of gas and dust. In time, the cloud started to spin, and became a disk with a bulge at the center. Gradually, the bulge got smaller and hotter, and eventually began to shine as the Sun. The gas and dust in the disk came together to form the planets.

PLANET EARTH Ancient peoples thought that the Earth was the center of the universe. But we now know that it is a mere planet—one of nine that circle the Sun in space. Among the planets, the Earth is quite small. Its diameter is only 7,926 miles (12,756 km) at the Equator. This is less than one-tenth the diameter of Jupiter. The Earth lies about 93 million miles (150 million km) from the Sun, and makes one journey around the Sun in $365\frac{1}{4}$ days (1 year). It spins around on its axis once every 24 hours (1 day).

What is special about the Earth?

Though it may be small, the Earth is without doubt one of the most beautiful bodies in space, as pictures taken from space show. Also it is unique among the planets in several respects. Most important, it supports life in thousands upon thousands of different forms—from tiny creatures too small for the eye to see, to giant trees and such huge animals as the elephant and whale. It is a watery planet. The water helps to support life and shape the surface. The Earth itself is alive. Its crust still ripples and splits with earthquakes. Volcanoes still erupt, disgorging molten rock from the Earth's interior.

What causes the seasons?

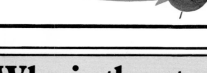

March 21
Spring in
N. Hemisphere

Autumn in
S. Hemisphere

December 21

June 21
Summer in
N. Hemisphere

Sun

Winter in
S. Hemisphere

September 21

Winter in
N. Hemisphere
Summer in
S. Hemisphere

Autumn in
N. Hemisphere

Spring in
S. Hemisphere

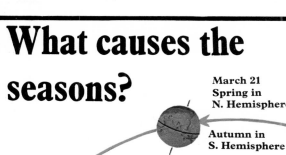

The regular changes in climate we call the *seasons* occur because the Earth's axis is tilted in relation to its path around the Sun. Places receive more or less heat according to whether they are tilted more towards or away from the Sun.

Why is the atmosphere so important?

The atmosphere is the thin layer of gases that surrounds the Earth. Though it is thin, it is very important. It gives us oxygen to breathe. Without oxygen, there could be little life on Earth. The atmosphere acts as a blanket to keep us warm at night when the Sun goes in. It filters out rays from the Sun that could burn us, and protects us from rocks from space.

What are the Northern and Southern lights?

In far northern and far southern regions of the world, nature puts on a splendid fireworks display. The night sky is lit up with flames and moving curtains of colored light. Such a display is called the *Northern Lights* in the north and the *Southern Lights* in the south. Its proper name is *aurora*. Aurorae are caused by particles from outer space hitting the atmosphere.

Can we see other planets with the naked eye?

You can see three of the planets very easily—Venus, Jupiter, and Mars. They shine like very bright stars. But unlike the stars, they wander across the celestial sphere month by month. The word *planet* means *wanderer*. You can also see Mercury and Saturn if you know where to look. But Uranus, Neptune, and Pluto are too faint to be seen.

The planets are the biggest members of the Sun's family, but compared with the Sun they are tiny. The Sun has 750 times more mass than all the planets put together! The planets are very different in appearance and make-up. That is what makes them so fascinating. Some of the other eight planets are smaller than the Earth. Others are bigger. None of them is much like the Earth. Those closer to the Sun become very much hotter than the Earth ever does. And those farther away get very much colder. They are not places where people from Earth could live.

October 1977

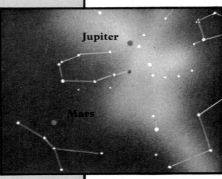

November 1977

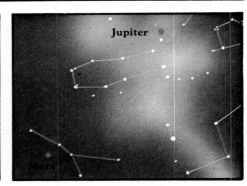

December 1977

Why do they shine?

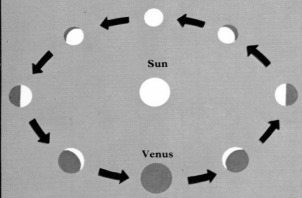

Phases of Venus as seen from Earth

The planets do not shine because they have their own light, as the Sun does. They shine because they reflect the Sun's light, just as the Moon does. And like the Moon, the planets appear to change shape, when viewed from the Earth. This is because we can see different amounts of the sunlit surface as the planet moves through the heavens.

What are the planets made of?

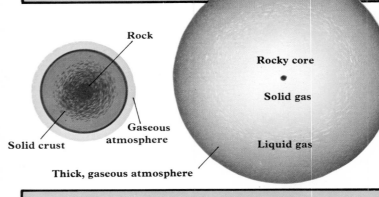

Rock

Rocky core

Solid gas

Liquid gas

Solid crust

Gaseous atmosphere

Thick, gaseous atmosphere

There is a great difference in make-up between the small planets and the giant ones. The small ones—Mercury, Venus, Earth, Mars, and Pluto—are made of rock. They have little, if any, atmosphere around them. The giant planets, Jupiter, Saturn, Uranus, and Neptune, are made up almost entirely of gas. This gas may exist as a liquid, or even a solid near the center of the planet.

Do they all have moons?

Saturn as seen from
one of its moons

**The 14 moons
of Jupiter**

Jupiter

Shadow
of a
moon

Do other suns
have planets?

The Sun is only one of thousands of millions of stars in the heavens. It would be very odd if it were the only one to have planets circling around it. Astronomers reckon that planetary systems are quite common. So there should be other planets like the Earth somewhere. But they would be too far away for us to see.

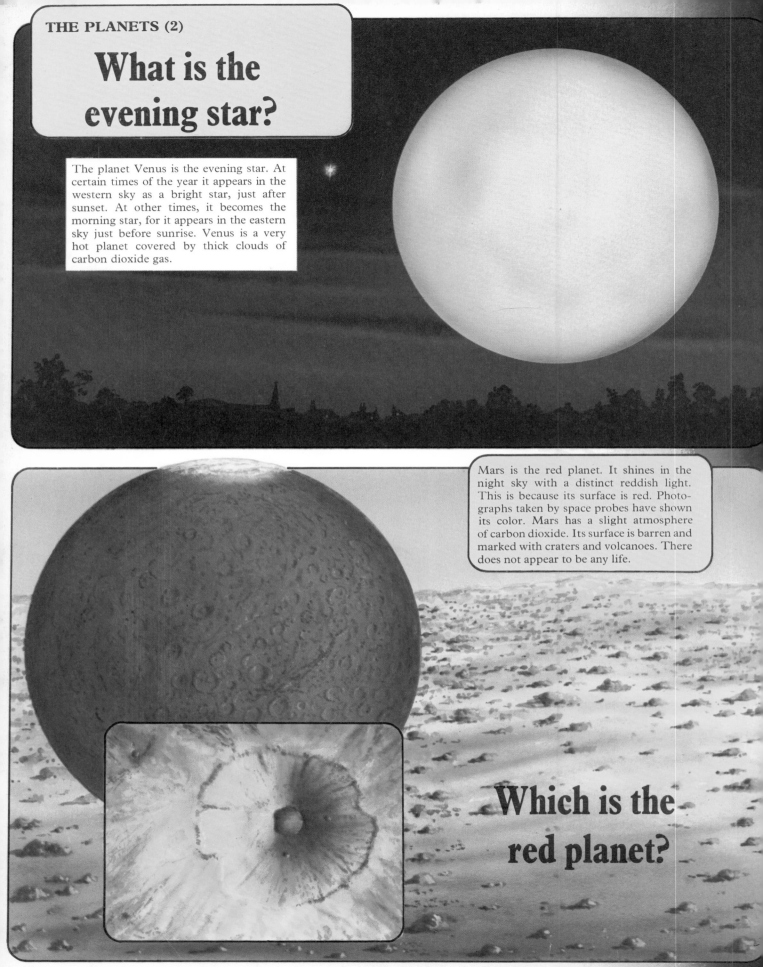

What is the evening star?

The planet Venus is the evening star. At certain times of the year it appears in the western sky as a bright star, just after sunset. At other times, it becomes the morning star, for it appears in the eastern sky just before sunrise. Venus is a very hot planet covered by thick clouds of carbon dioxide gas.

Mars is the red planet. It shines in the night sky with a distinct reddish light. This is because its surface is red. Photographs taken by space probes have shown its color. Mars has a slight atmosphere of carbon dioxide. Its surface is barren and marked with craters and volcanoes. There does not appear to be any life.

Which is the red planet?

Which is the giant planet?

Jupiter is the giant planet. If it were the size of a football, then the Earth would be only the size of a marble. Through a telescope, Jupiter shows a disk crossed with parallel dark and light bands. These are thought to be the tops of clouds in its thick hydrogen atmosphere. They form bands because the planet is spinning around very fast.

What is the red spot?

The red spot is a huge oval mark often visible in the southern part of Jupiter's disk. It is thought to be caused by a gigantic storm that has been raging on the planet for many centuries. Other spots and marks appear on Jupiter from time to time, but they are not so distinctive.

Which is the ringed planet?

Saturn is known as the ringed planet because a set of flat rings surrounds it at the equator. Only two of the four rings are bright. We can see them at different angles, year by year. They are probably made of ice and dust, and are very thin. They almost disappear from view when we look at them edge-on.

ROCKS AND DUST We tend to think that the space between the Sun, the planets, and their moons is empty. But it is not. Scattered over the solar system are clouds of dust and frozen gas and lumps of rock of all shapes and sizes. Usually, we cannot see such bodies because they are too tiny. But occasionally some of them approach close enough to us to shine quite brightly. Some even come so close to the Earth that its gravity plucks them from space, and they fall to the ground.

What are comets?

Comet disappears

Sun

Comet appears

Tail pointing away from Sun

One of the most spectacular of all the sights in the heavens is a bright comet. Comets are great masses of dust and frozen gas which glow when they approach the Sun. The brightest ones can even be seen in daylight.

Do comets reappear?

Like all members of the Sun's family, comets travel in a regular path, around and around the Sun. Most of them have so far to travel that they do not reappear for thousands of years. But some do. The most famous is Halley's comet, which reappears every 76 years or so.

Bayeux Tapestry

The comet we know as *Halley's comet* has been seen many times over the years. It reappeared, for example, in 1066, at about the time of the Battle of Hastings. It is shown on the Bayeux tapestry, which commemorates William the Conqueror's victory over the English.

What are asteroids?

The asteroids are the largest of the rocky lumps in the solar system. They circle in a broad belt between the planets Mars and Jupiter. The biggest, called *Ceres*, is about 470 miles (750 km) across.

What are meteors?

When bits of rock are captured by the Earth, they plunge through the upper air. There, they are heated up by friction and start to burn. From the ground, this shows up as a fiery streak, which we call a *meteor*.

What are meteorites?

Most of the bits of rock that cause meteors burn up into dust. But some are big enough to reach the ground. We call them *meteorites*. Some are made up mainly of iron and nickel, not rock.

Where is the largest crater?

If a meteorite is very large, it makes a huge hole, or crater, when it hits the ground. A few craters can still be found on Earth. The biggest, in Arizona, measures 4,150 feet (1,265 meters) across, and is 575 feet (175 meters) deep in places. Most Moon craters were caused by the impact of meteorites.

How far away are the stars?

Our star, the Sun, lies 93 million miles (150 million km) away. The next nearest star lies over 25 million million miles (40 million million km) away. It is called *Proxima Centauri*. Its light takes some $4\frac{1}{3}$ years to travel to the Earth. We say it lies $4\frac{1}{3}$ light-years away.

THE DISTANT STARS Gazing at the stars is endlessly interesting. Even with the naked eye, we can see that they are not all alike. Most of them are white. Others are tinged yellow, red, orange, blue or green. Some stars seem much brighter than others. This is because they lie at different distances from us, and the farther away they are, the fainter they appear. Many of the stars are only about as bright as the Sun. But some are tens of thousands of times brighter.

What are they made of?

Like the Sun, a star is made up mostly of hydrogen gas. This gas fuels the star's nuclear furnace, which produces its heat and light. Stars also contain traces of some of the other chemical elements found on Earth, including iron.

Why do stars twinkle?

On most nights when you look at the stars, you notice that they seem to twinkle. But the twinkling has nothing to do with the stars. It happens because layers of air at different temperatures bend starlight this way and that as it passes through the atmosphere.

How many stars are there?

If you were very patient, you might be able to count about 5,000 stars in the sky with the naked eye. Through binoculars or a telescope, you would see many thousands more. Altogether astronomers estimate there are at least 100,000 million in the star system our Sun belongs to.

Do the stars shine steadily?

Ignoring twinkling, most stars shine steadily year in, year out. But some vary in brightness regularly. They are called *variable stars*. Stars called *novae* (new stars) suddenly flare up and then fade again. Others, called *supernovae*, flare up so violently they blast themselves apart.

Surface of supergiant

How big are they?

White dwarf

Sun

There are very wide differences in the sizes of stars. The Sun, which measures about 865,000 miles (1.4 million km) across, is of average size. There are stars called *white dwarfs* which are very much smaller—only a few thousand miles across. And there are *giant stars* tens of times bigger than the Sun, and *supergiant stars* hundreds of times bigger.

Giant star

What is a double star?

A *double star* is one which on closer inspection turns out to be two stars close together. They may only appear close together but actually be far apart. Or they may really be close together. Then they form a *binary system*.

Is the space between the stars empty?

Vast distances separate the stars in the heavens. But this space is not completely empty. It contains small amounts of dust and gas. In places, thicker clouds of dust and gas appear. We call them *nebulae* ("clouds"). Some nebulae shine brightly. Others appear dark, because they block the light of stars behind them.

STAR GROUPS The patterns of bright stars we call the constellations help us find our way through the heavens. The stars in the constellations appear to lie close together in space. But this is not really the case. They lie at different distances, and only appear close together because they are in the same direction when we look at them. However, stars do congregate together in space. In fact only one star in every three journeys through space alone. The Sun is one of them. On a wider scale, all the stars you see in the sky belong to the same star system, or galaxy. And on a wider scale still, galaxies tend to group together in space.

What is a star cluster?

In a binary star system, the two stars revolve around each other. There are also *multiple star systems* in which three or more stars circle around each other. On a larger scale, tens and even hundreds of stars may cluster together in space to form loose *open clusters*. Sometimes several thousand stars form a closely packed *globular cluster*.

What is the Milky Way?

On dark nights, you often see a faint band of light arcing across the sky. We call it the *Milky Way*. If you look at it with binoculars, you see that it consists of thousands of stars. It represents a slice through our galaxy.

What is our galaxy like?

We also call our galaxy the *Milky Way*. It is a huge disk of stars, which has a dense center and has arms curving out from it. The whole disk revolves, somewhat like a pinwheel. From one side to the other, our galaxy measures about one million million million miles, or about 100,000 light-years.

Are all galaxies the same?

Our own galaxy has curved arms coming from a dense center. It is called a *spiral galaxy*. There are many spiral galaxies in the universe. Some galaxies have no distinct arms, and are called *elliptical* (oval) *galaxies*. Other galaxies are shapeless, or *irregular*.

THE OUTER GALAXIES Millions upon millions of miles beyond our own galaxy—the Milky Way—lie other galaxies. Many of them are similar to our own, and contain a similar number of stars—about 100,000 million. They are, on average, about the same size too—about 100,000 light-years in diameter. They also contain the same kinds of heavenly bodies as our own galaxy. Space and all the galaxies within it make up what we call the universe. Some of the galaxies astronomers can see through their telescopes are so far away that their light takes thousands of millions of years to reach us. This means that we are seeing them as they were thousands of millions of years ago.

Can we see any with the naked eye?

Most galaxies are so far away that they can be seen only through telescopes. But one or two are just visible to the naked eye. One is the famous Andromeda galaxy. This is visible as a misty patch in the constellation of Andromeda. It is often called the *Andromeda Nebula*.

Which is the closest?

The closest galaxy lies in the far southern heavens. It is clearly visible as a distinct cloud. And it is called the *Large Magellanic Cloud*. Nearby is the *Small Magellanic Cloud*, another close galaxy. They are named after the famous Portuguese navigator Ferdinand Magellan.

Are the galaxies moving?

Everything in the universe moves. The stars spin around the center of their galaxy. And the galaxy moves bodily through space. Viewed from the Earth, almost all the galaxies appear to be moving away from us. The farthest appear to be traveling fastest.

How did the universe begin?

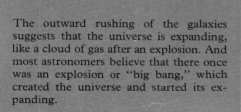

The outward rushing of the galaxies suggests that the universe is expanding, like a cloud of gas after an explosion. And most astronomers believe that there once was an explosion or "big bang," which created the universe and started its expanding.

STUDYING THE HEAVENS (1) We can learn quite a bit about the stars and the planets just by looking at them with the naked eye and plotting their positions in the heavens. But to study them in detail, we have to use instruments. The most useful of all the astronomer's instruments is the telescope. This is a much better collector of light than the human eye. It can detect stars too faint for the eye to see, and can show some details of the planets. Astronomers use other instruments to unravel the secrets starlight holds. They also learn much about the stars from the radio waves stars give out.

Where do astronomers work?

What kinds of telescopes do they use?

Astronomers use two main kinds of telescopes. They differ in the way they collect and focus the light from the stars. One kind uses mirrors. It is called a *reflector*. The other kind uses lenses. It is called a *refractor*. Reflectors are by far the most important of the two. This one is the 200-inch (508-cm) reflector at Palomar Observatory in California.

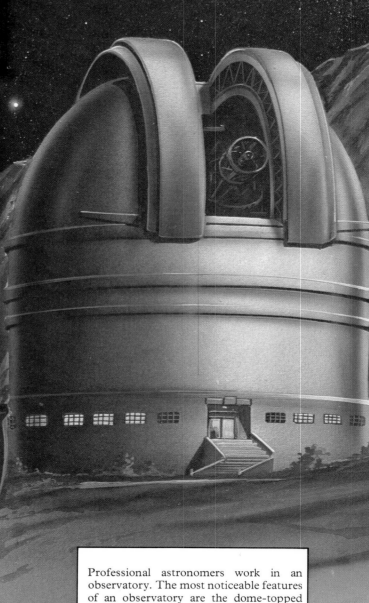

Professional astronomers work in an observatory. The most noticeable features of an observatory are the dome-topped buildings which house the telescopes. The domes roll back at night to expose the telescopes. Most major observatories are located away from the cities, high up in the mountains in sunny climates. There, the air is thinner and free from dust. This enables much clearer viewing.

How do reflectors work?

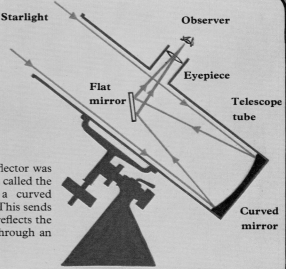

The most important type of reflector was devised by Isaac Newton, and is called the *Newtonian reflector*. It uses a curved mirror to gather the light rays. This sends the rays to a flat mirror, which reflects the light into the observer's eyes through an eyepiece.

How do refractors work?

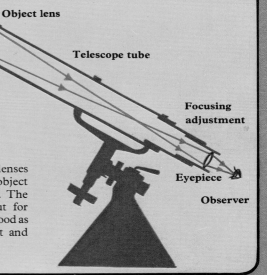

The refractor consists of two sets of lenses held in a tube. At the front is the object lens and at the rear is the eyepiece. The eyepiece can be moved in and out for focusing. Most refractors are not as good as reflectors because they absorb light and may distort the image.

Are binoculars any use in astronomy?

Binoculars are very useful—especially for the amateur astronomer. They are inexpensive, and enable the observer to see many more interesting objects than can be seen with the naked eye. The Moon is a great sight through binoculars. And binoculars are ideal for comet watching. Many comets have been found recently by amateurs with binoculars.

Why is photography important in astronomy?

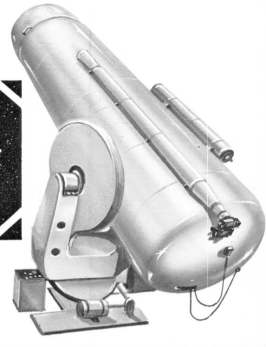

Astronomers at the big observatories rarely look through their telescopes. Instead, they use them as big cameras to take photographs of the night sky. Photographic film stores the light that falls on it, so if you point a telescope at the same part of the sky for hours on end, very faint stars will make their mark on the film.

What does starlight tell us?

Spectral lines

Spectrum

Prism

Star-light

Telescope

Astronomers can make starlight tell us a great deal. They pass it through a prism in an instrument called a *spectroscope*. The prism splits the starlight into a *spectrum*, or band of color, crossed by dark lines. From the nature of these lines, astronomers can tell how hot the star is, how fast it spins, and many other things.

Spectrum of Sirius

Spectrum of Sun

At the Planetarium

If you are interested in astronomy, you should go to a planetarium. There, you will see how and why the stars change from season to season; how the planets and the Moon move through the heavens; and many other things. You sit in a chamber with a domed roof, onto which all the heavenly bodies can be projected.

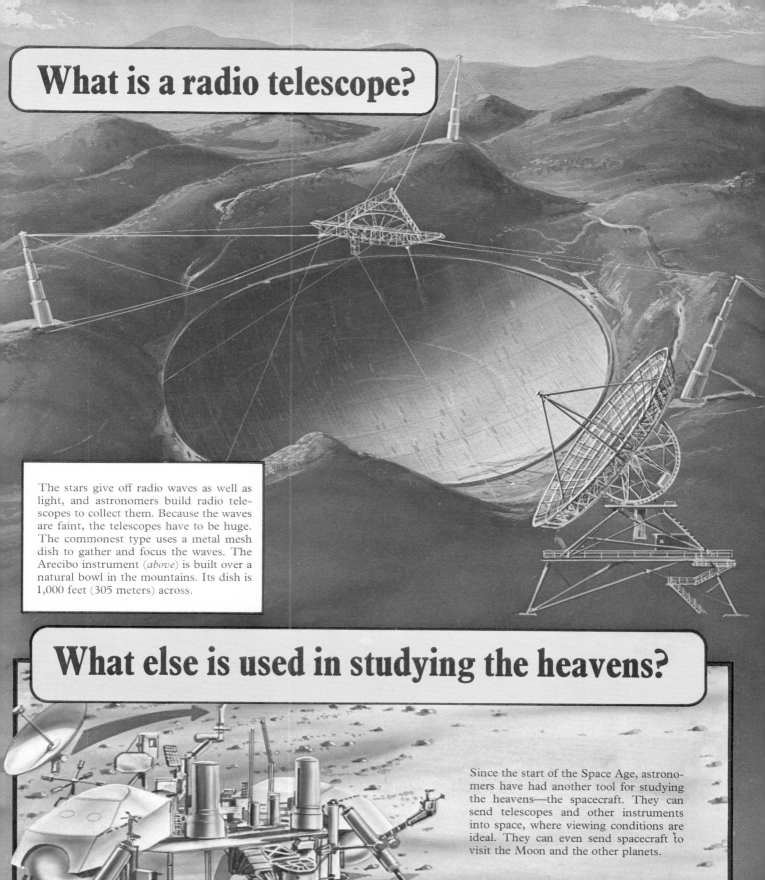

What is a radio telescope?

The stars give off radio waves as well as light, and astronomers build radio telescopes to collect them. Because the waves are faint, the telescopes have to be huge. The commonest type uses a metal mesh dish to gather and focus the waves. The Arecibo instrument (*above*) is built over a natural bowl in the mountains. Its dish is 1,000 feet (305 meters) across.

What else is used in studying the heavens?

Since the start of the Space Age, astronomers have had another tool for studying the heavens—the spacecraft. They can send telescopes and other instruments into space, where viewing conditions are ideal. They can even send spacecraft to visit the Moon and the other planets.

A-Z of Stars and Planets

A

Andromeda A constellation.
Aquarius, the Water-Bearer. A constellation.
Aquila, the Eagle. A constellation.
Ara, the Altar. A constellation.
Aries, the Ram. A constellation.
artificial satellite An artificial object that circles around the Earth in space.
asteroid A tiny planet-like body that circles around the Sun.
astrology Studying the stars to try to foretell the future.
astronaut A space traveler; literally "startraveler."
atmosphere The layer of gases around a heavenly body.
Auriga, the Charioteer. A constellation.
aurora A glow that appears in far northern and southern night skies. Commonly called the northern or southern lights.

B

Böotes, the Herdsman. A constellation.

C

calendar A means of splitting up time; it organizes the days, weeks, and months into years.
Cancer, the Crab. A constellation.
Canis Major, the Great Dog. A constellation.
Canis Minor, the Little Dog. A constellation.
Capricornus, the Sea Goat. A constellation.
Carina, the Keel. A constellation.
Cassiopeia A constellation.
celestial sphere An imaginary globe surrounding the Earth, to which all the stars appear to be fixed.
Centaurus, the Centaur. A constellation.
Cetus, the Whale. A constellation.
comet A ball of dust and gas that circles the Sun.
constellation A pattern bright stars make in the sky.
cosmic rays Streams of particles that bombard the Earth from space.
cosmos Another word for "universe."
crater A hole made when a lump of rock from space hits a planet or a moon.

Crux, the Southern Cross. A constellation.
Cygnus, the Swan. A constellation.

D

double star A star that looks like a single star to the eye, but is actually made up of two stars close together.
Draco, the Dragon. A constellation.

E

eclipse What happens when one heavenly body passes in front of another and blots out its light.
equinox One of two times of the year when the lengths of the day and night are equal. The vernal (spring) equinox occurs on about March 21st, and the autumnal equinox occurs on about September 23rd.
Eridanus A constellation.

G

galaxy A great spinning star island in space.
Gemini, the Twins. A constellation.
gravity A powerful force which makes bodies attract one another. The Earth's gravity keeps us firmly on the ground.

H

Hercules A constellation.
horoscope A diagram used in astrology showing the positions of the heavenly bodies when a person was born.
Hydra, the Water Serpent. A constellation.

I

interstellar space Space outside the solar system and among the stars.

L

Leo, the Lion. A constellation.
Libra, the Scales. A constellation.
light-year The distance light travels in a year—about 6 million million miles or 10 million million km.
lunar Of the Moon.
Lyra, the Lyre. A constellation.

M

magnitude A scale of star brightness. The brightest stars you can see with the naked eye are of the 1st magnitude; the faintest are of the 6th magnitude.
mare One of the dark areas on the Moon; means "sea."
meteor A streak of light in the sky, caused when tiny rocks burn up in the Earth's atmosphere.
moon A body that orbits around a planet; properly called "satellite."

N

nebula A cloud of dust and gas in space.
nova A faint star that suddenly flares up and appears "new."
nuclear reaction A process in which atoms either split or combine together, producing tremendous energy. Stars get their energy when hydrogen atoms combine.

O

observatory A place where astronomers study the stars.
Ophiuchus, the Serpent Bearer. A constellation.
orbit The path in space of a body when it travels around another.
Orion A constellation.

P

Pegasus, the Winged Horse. A constellation.
period An interval of time between the beginning and end of something, such as an orbit.
Perseus A constellation.
phase The apparent change in shape of the Moon or a planet as more or less of its surface is lit by the Sun.
Pisces, the Fishes. A constellation.
Plough The name for the pattern made by the seven brightest stars in the constellation Ursa Major.
pole star The star Polaris, which lies almost directly above the north pole and does not appear to move.
pulsar A tiny star that gives out its energy in rapid bursts or pulses.
Puppis, the Poop. A constellation.

Q

quasar A mysterious, distant heavenly body that gives out powerful radio waves.

R

radio astronomy A branch of astronomy which studies the radio waves stars and galaxies give out.

red giant A huge, cool red star that may be hundreds of times bigger than the Sun.

reflector A telescope that collects light with a curved mirror.

refractor A telescope that collects light with lenses.

S

Sagittarius, the Archer. A constellation.

satellite A small body that circles around a planet; a moon.

season A regular change in climate that occurs because the Earth's axis is tilted in space.

Serpens, the Serpent. A constellation.

Scorpio, the Scorpion. A constellation.

shooting star Another term for meteor.

solar Of the Sun.

solstice A time of the year when the Sun appears farthest north or south of the Equator. In northern parts of the Earth, for example, it is mid-summer when the Sun appears farthest north (about June 21st); it is mid-winter when the Sun appears farthest south (December 21st).

spectrum The band of color formed when light passes through a prism. Astronomers can tell much about a star from the spectrum of its light.

stellar Of the stars.

sundial A kind of clock that tells time according to the position of the Sun.

supergiant A huge star many hundreds or even thousands of times bigger than the Sun.

supernova A star that flares up brilliantly as it explodes.

T

Taurus, the Bull. A constellation.

telescope An instrument for observing distant objects, such as the stars and planets.

terrestrial Of the Earth.

tides The regular rise and fall of the oceans caused by the Moon's gravity.

transit The passage of Mercury or Venus across the disk of the Sun.

U

universe All that exists—space and all the bodies within it.

Ursa Major, the Great Bear. A constellation.

Ursa Minor, the Little Bear. A constellation.

V

Vela, the Sails. A constellation.

Virgo, the Virgin. A constellation.

W

white dwarf A tiny but very heavy star that is near the end of its life.

Z

zodiac A band of the heavens through which the Sun and the planets appear to move during the year. The signs of the zodiac are the signs of the constellations the band passes through.

Famous Astronomers

Aristarchus (200 BC) Greek who first proposed that the Earth travels around the Sun.

Brahe, Tycho (1546–1601) Great Danish observer who built a famous observatory on Hveen, in the Baltic.

Copernicus, Nicolaus (1473–1543) Polish priest-astronomer who founded modern astronomy with his idea of a Sun-centered universe.

Einstein, Albert (1879–1955) German physicist who put forward the theory of relativity that changed our ideas of space, time, and motion.

Galileo (1564–1642) Italian who first used a telescope to observe the heavens.

Halley, Edmond (1656–1742) Englishman particularly famed for his studies of comets, including the one named after him.

Herschel, William (1738–1822) German-born astronomer who settled in England; discovered the planet Uranus in 1781.

Hipparchus (100 BC) The greatest Greek astronomer, who drew up star catalogues and discovered trigonometry.

Hoyle, Fred (1915–   ) English astronomer best known for his "steady-state" theory of the origin of the universe.

Hubble, Edwin (1899–1953) American who pioneered the study of the outer galaxies.

Jansky, Karl (1905–1950) American radio engineer who first detected radio waves from the heavens, and thus founded radio astronomy.

Kepler, Johannes (1571–1630) German who first described how the planets moved—in ellipses.

Lemaître, Georges (1894–1966) One of the first to develop the "big-bang" theory about how the universe began.

Messier, Charles (1730–1817) Frenchman who compiled a list of nebulae and clusters. Many are still identified by their M-numbers.

Newton, Isaac (1642–1727) Brilliant Englishman who discovered the laws of gravity and motion and built the first reflecting telescope.

Ptolemy (AD 150's) Greek who wrote the first astronomical work, the *Almagest* ("The Greatest").

Schiaparelli, Giovanni (1835–1910) Italian who said he observed canals on Mars, which led people to believe that there might be life on that planet.

THE SOLAR SYSTEM

Name	Distance from Sun miles (km)	Diameter at Equator miles (km)	Density (water = 1)	*Turns on axis in	†Circles Sun in
Sun	—	865,000 (1,392,000)	1.4	25 days	—
Moon	—	2,160 (3,476)	3.3	27 days	—
Mercury	36,000,000 (58,000,000)	3,015 (4,850)	5.4	59 days	88 days
Venus	67,000,000 (108,000,000)	7,545 (12,140)	5.2	244 days	225 days
Earth	93,000,000 (150,000,000)	7,926 (12,756)	5.5	23h 56min	365¼ days
Mars	142,000,000 (228,000,000)	4,220 (6,790)	4.0	24h 37min	687 days
Jupiter	484,000,000 (778,000,000)	88,600 (142,600)	1.3	9h 50min	12 years
Saturn	887,000,000 (1,427,000,000)	74,700 (120,200)	0.7	10h 14min	30 years
Uranus	1,783,000,000 (2,870,000,000)	30,500 (49,000)	1.6	10h 49min	84 years
Neptune	2,794,000,000 (4,497,000,000)	31,200 (50,200)	2.3	15h 48min	165 years
Pluto	3,670,000,000 (5,900,000,000)	3,980 (6,400)	?	6 days	248 years

* This is the planet's day.   † This is the planet's year.

THE BRIGHTEST STARS

Name	Constellation	Distance (light-years)
Sirius	Canis Major	9
Canopus	Carina	200
Rigil Kent	Centaurus	4⅓
Arcturus	Boötes	40
Vega	Lyra	30
Capella	Auriga	50
Rigel	Orion	800
Procyon	Canis Minor	11
Achernar	Eridanus	130
Hadar	Centaurus	400
Altair	Aquila	16
Betelgeuse	Orion	650

THE NEAREST STARS

Name	Constellation	Distance (light-years)
Proxima Centauri	Centaurus	4.3
Rigil Kent	Centaurus	4.4
Barnard's Star	Ophiuchus	5.9
Wolf 359	Leo	7.6
Lalande 21185	Ursa Major	8.1
Sirius	Canis Major	8.8

NAMES OF THE CONSTELLATIONS

Latin name	English name	Latin name	English name	Latin name	English name
Andromeda	Andromeda	Delphinus	Dolphin	Pegasus	Pegasus (winged horse)
Antlia	Air Pump	Dorado	Swordfish		
Apus	Bird of Paradise	Draco	Dragon	Perseus	Perseus
Aquarius	Water Bearer	Equuleus	Little Horse	Phoenix	Phoenix
Aquila	Eagle	Eridanus	River Eridanus	Pictor	Painter (or Easel)
Ara	Altar	Fornax	Furnace	Pisces	Fishes
Aries	Ram	Gemini	Twins	Piscis Austrinus	Southern Fish
Auriga	Charioteer	Grus	Crane	Puppis	Poop
Boötes	Herdsman	Hercules	Hercules	Pyxis	Mariner's Compass
Caelum	Chisel	Horologium	Clock	Reticulum	Net
Camelopardus	Giraffe	Hydra	Sea-Serpent	Sagitta	Arrow
Cancer	Crab	Hydrus	Watersnake	Sagittarius	Archer
Canes Venatici	Hunting Dogs	Indus	Indian	Scorpius	Scorpion
Canis Major	Great Dog	Lacerta	Lizard	Sculptor	Sculptor
Canis Minor	Little Dog	Leo	Lion	Scutum	Shield
Capricornus	Sea-Goat	Leo Minor	Little Lion	Serpens	Serpent
Carina	Keel	Lepus	Hare	Sextans	Sextant
Cassiopeia	Cassiopeia	Libra	Scales	Taurus	Bull
Centaurus	Centaur	Lupus	Wolf	Telescopium	Telescope
Cepheus	Cepheus	Lynx	Lynx	Triangulum	Triangle
Cetus	Whale	Lyra	Lyre	Triangulum Australe	Southern Triangle
Chamaeleon	Chameleon	Mensa	Table		
Circinus	Pair of Compasses	Microscopium	Microscope	Tucana	Toucan
Columba	Dove	Monoceros	Unicorn	Ursa Major	Great Bear (or Plough)
Coma Berenices	Berenice's Hair	Musca	Fly		
Corona Australis	Southern Crown	Norma	Rule	Ursa Minor	Little Bear
Corona Borealis	Northern Crown	Octans	Octant	Vela	Sails
Corvus	Crow	Ophiuchus	Serpent Bearer	Virgo	Virgin
Crater	Cup	Orion	Orion (hunter)	Volans	Flying Fish
Crux	Southern Cross	Pavo	Peacock	Vulpecula	Fox
Cygnus	Swan				

Index

Lerner Publications Company
241 First Avenue North, Minneapolis, Minnesota 55401